Contents

School and home

▼ **Our school is on Rydal Street, in a town called Darlington.**

Everyone in our class lives in Darlington, but our homes are all in different places.

school   street   town   homes

Start-Up
Connections

JOURNEY TO SCHOOL

Anna Lee

Evans Brothers Limited

First published in this edition in 2010

Published by Evans Brothers Limited
2A Portman Mansions
Chiltern Street
London W1U 6NR

Produced for Evans Brothers Limited by
White-Thomson Publishing Ltd.,
+44 (0) 843 2087 460
www.wtpub.co.uk

Printed & bound in China by New Era Printing
Company Limited

Editor: Dereen Taylor
Consultants: Nina Siddall, Head of Primary School
Improvement, East Sussex; Norah Granger, former
primary head teacher and senior lecturer in Education,
University of Brighton; Kate Ruttle, freelance literacy
consultant and Literacy Co-ordinator, Special Needs
Co-ordinator, and Deputy Headteacher at a primary
school in Suffolk.
Designer: Leishman Design
Cover design: Balley Design Limited

British Library Cataloguing in Publication Data

Lee, Anna.
    Journey to school. -- (Start-up connections)
    1. Urban transportation--Juvenile literature. 2. School
    children--Transportation--Juvenile literature.
    I. Title II. Series
    388.4-dc22

ISBN: 978 0 237 54173 6

Picture acknowledgements
All photographs by Chris Fairclough except Royal Mail
Group plc 8; Alan Towse 9.

Acknowledgements
The publishers would like to thank staff, students and
parents at Dodmire Infant School, Darlington, for their
involvement in the preparation of this book.

◄ **Shirley lives in a house close to school.**

► **Alex lives in a flat a long way away.**

Every home has a different address.

Looking at addresses

◀ Shirley has just received a letter from her friend in France.

The postman delivered it to her house.

The letter has her address on it.

France postman delivered

▼ **The first line of the address tells us her house number and the name of her street.**

Shirley Lim
21 Falmar Road
Darlington
County Durham DH1 2CN
UK

The second line tells us what town Shirley lives in.

The third line tells us her county and her postcode.

What street does Shirley live in?

county   postcode

Why do we need addresses?

▼ We need addresses so that the post office knows where to deliver our post.

post office

▼ When we travel, we put our address on our luggage.

This means that if the luggage is lost, the person who finds it can return it to our home.

What is your address?

travel luggage

A plan of our school

Plans **help us to find our way around places that are new to us.**

▶ **This is a plan of our school.**

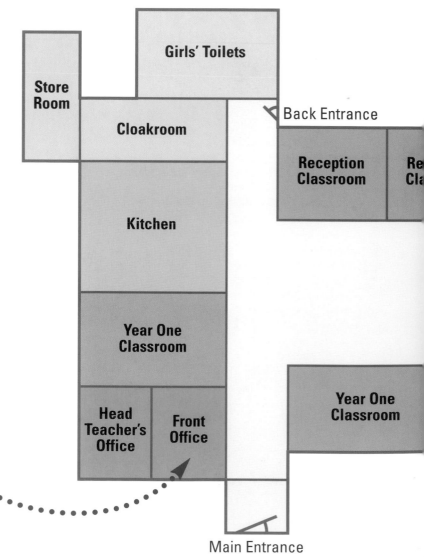

Store Room

Girls' Toilets

Cloakroom

Back Entrance

Reception Classroom

Re Cla

Kitchen

Year One Classroom

Head Teacher's Office

Front Office

Year One Classroom

Main Entrance

plan   around

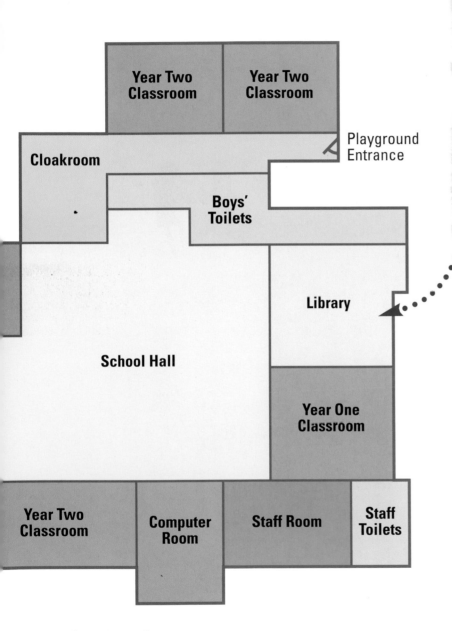

Year Two Classroom

Year Two Classroom

Cloakroom

Playground Entrance

Boys' Toilets

Library

School Hall

Year One Classroom

Year Two Classroom

Computer Room

Staff Room

Staff Toilets

Outside walls

Inside walls

Visitors to the school can look at it to help them find different rooms.

Which rooms are next to the computer room?

computer room

Our local area

Maps **help us to find our way around our** local area.

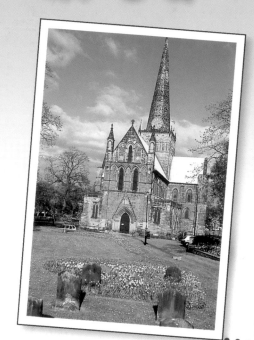

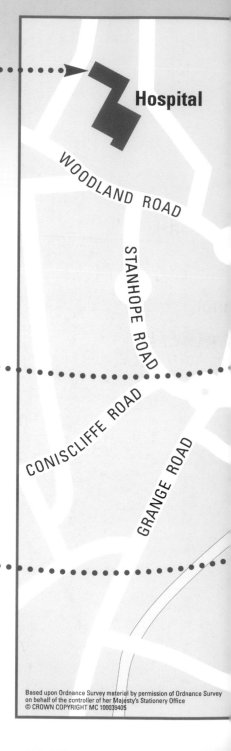

Hospital

WOODLAND ROAD

STANHOPE ROAD

CONISCLIFFE ROAD

GRANGE ROAD

Based upon Ordnance Survey material by permission of Ordnance Survey on behalf of the controller of her Majesty's Stationery Office
© CROWN COPYRIGHT MC 100039405

▶ Here is a map of the area around our school.

It shows some of the buildings.

maps   local area   buildings

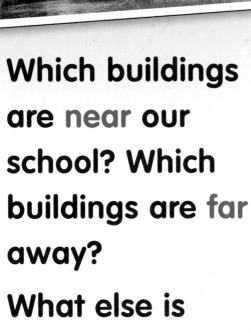

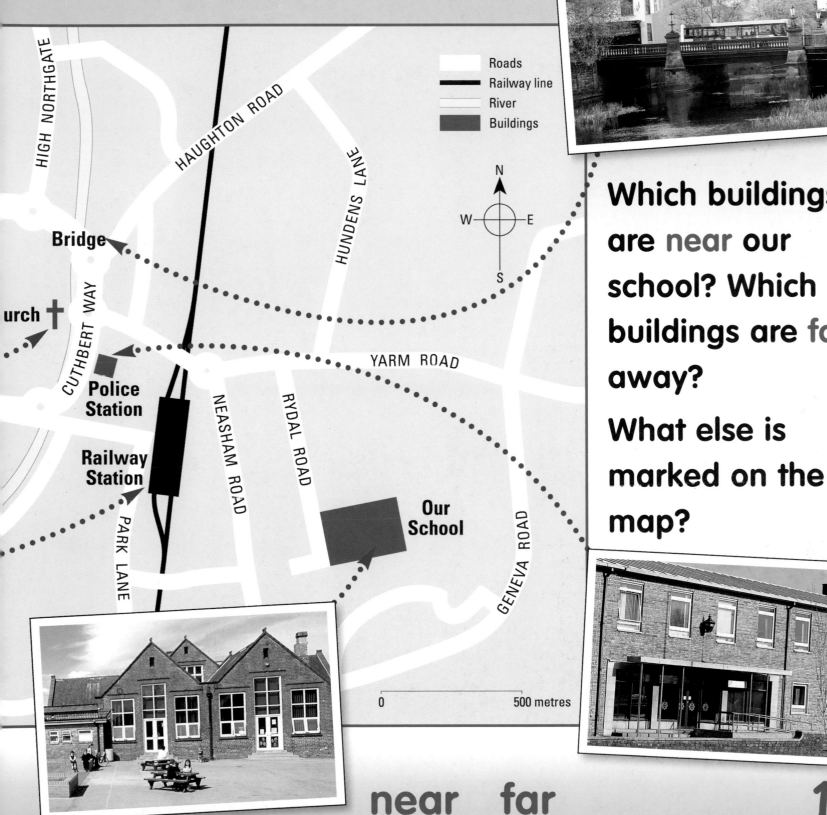

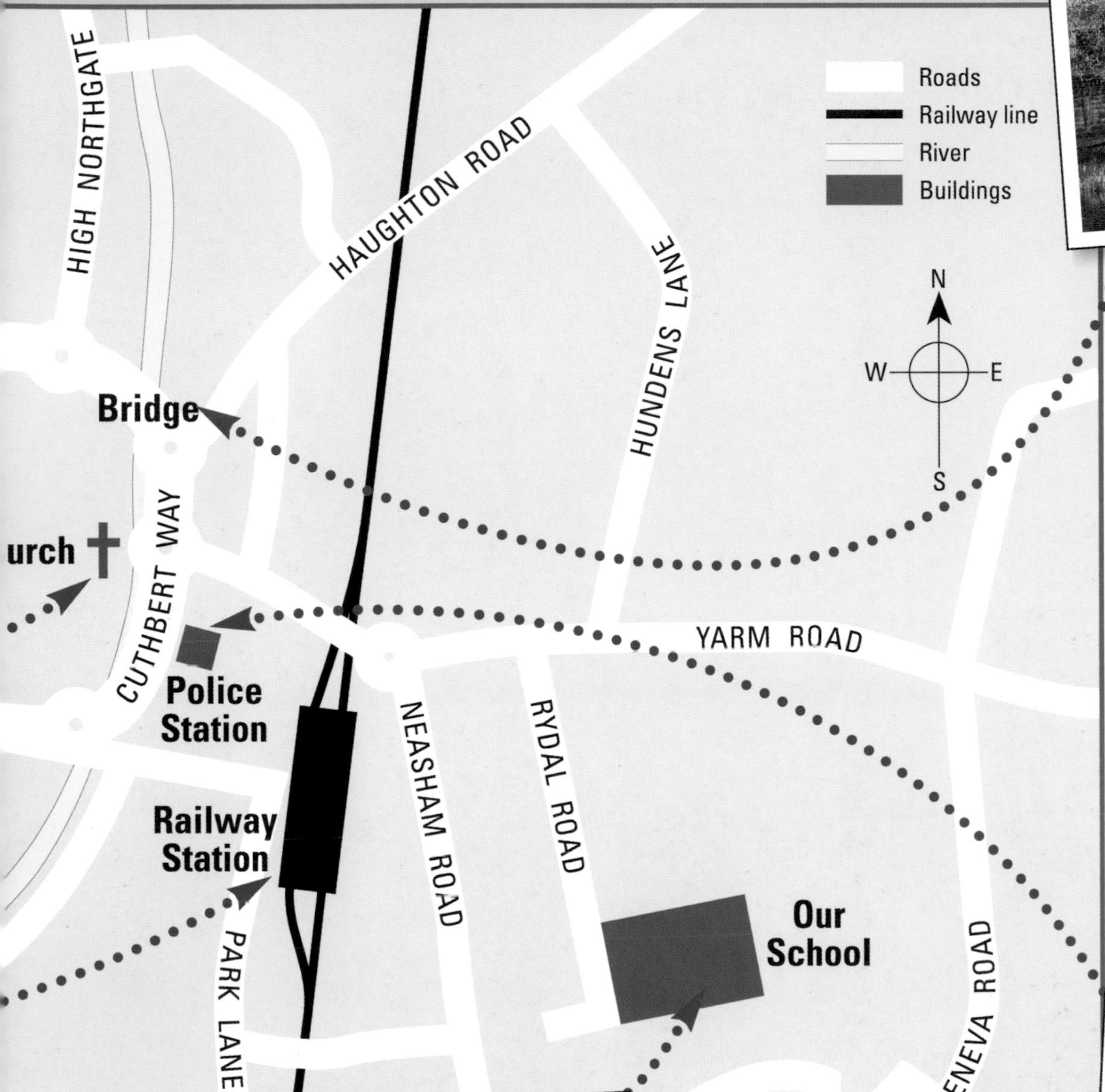
Roads
Railway line
River
Buildings
N
S
W
E
HIGH NORTHGATE
HAUGHTON ROAD
HUNDENS LANE
Bridge
urch
CUTHBERT WAY
Police Station
Railway Station
YARM ROAD
NEASHAM ROAD
RYDAL ROAD
PARK LANE
GENEVA ROAD
Our School
0
500 metres

Which buildings are near our school? Which buildings are far away?

What else is marked on the map?

near far

Going to school

▶ Our school is close to Georgina's house.

She **walks** to school with her sister and mother.

◀ Zac lives further away. He **rides** his **bike** to school with his dad.

What are they wearing for **safety**?

walks   rides   bike   safety

► Shirley catches the bus to school with her brother, her sister and her dad.

There are many bus stops on the bus route.

◄ This bus stop is outside the post office.

How do you get to school?

What buildings do you pass on your journey?

bus   route   journey

Alex's route to school

Alex lives the **furthest** from school.

▲ **His grand-mother drives him in her car.**

▶ **They drive past the petrol station ...**

▶ **... under the railway bridge ...**

furthest   drives   past   under   left

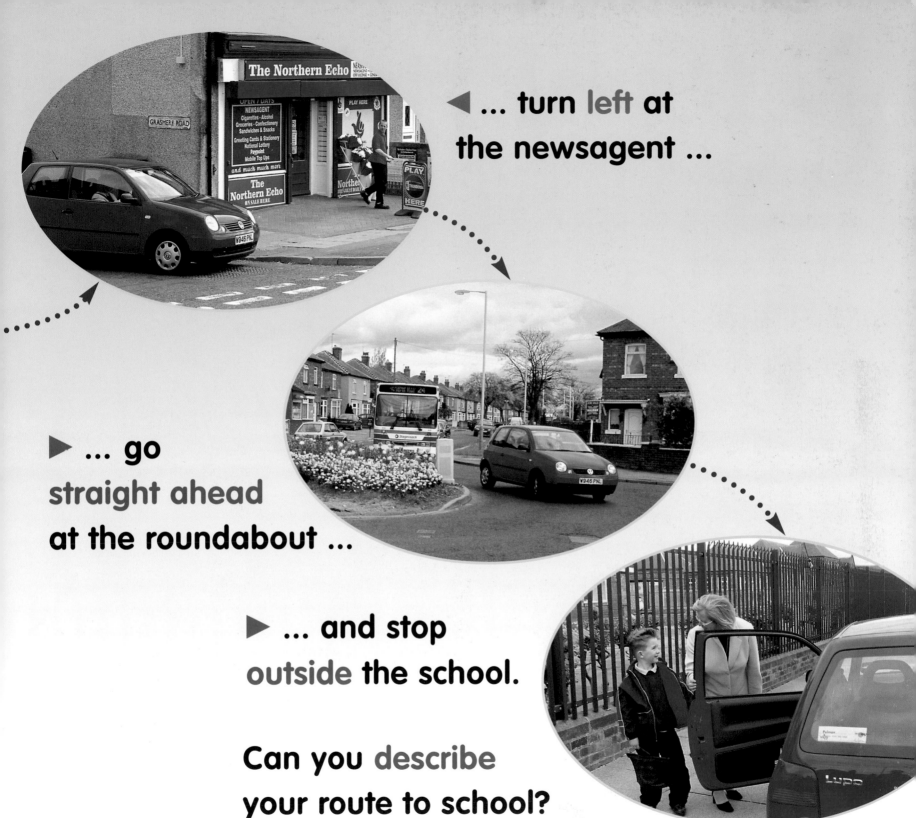

◀ ... turn left at the newsagent ...

▶ ... go straight ahead at the roundabout ...

▶ ... and stop outside the school.

Can you describe your route to school?

straight ahead   outside   describe   **17**

A travel pictogram

▶ Fiona drew a pictogram of all the different ways children in our class get to school.

▲ She typed in the information ...

▲ ... and used the mouse to draw a pictogram.

pictogram

▼ **The bottom of the pictogram shows the different ways pupils come to school.**

The number of symbols tell us how many children use each method of transport.

How many children walk to school?

How many come by bus?

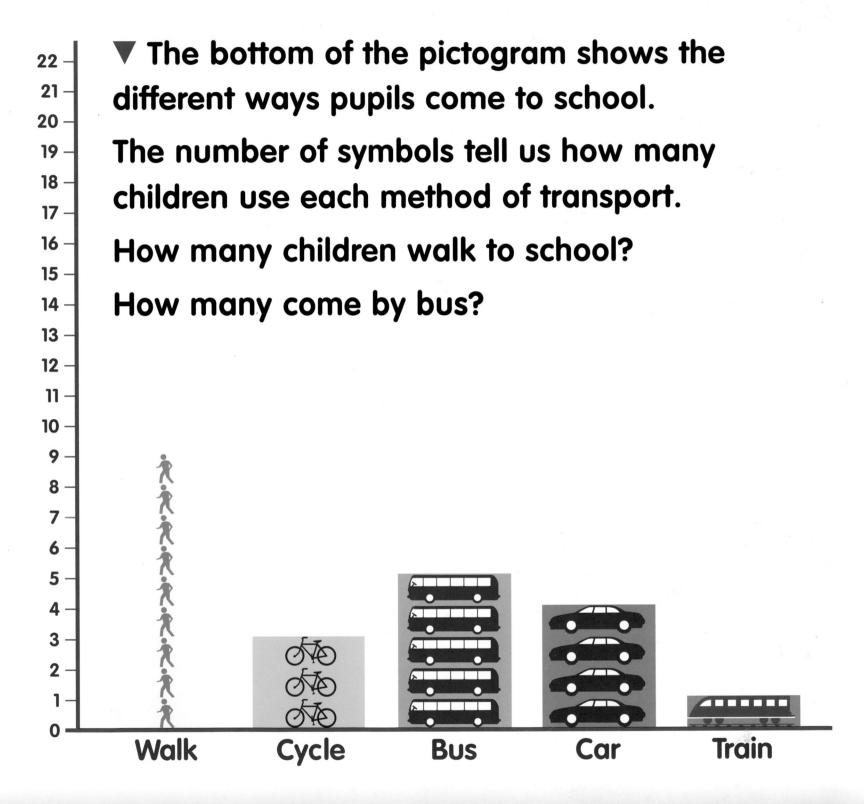

Shirley's journey to school

▶ This map is similar to the one on pages 12-13. This time more places in our local area are marked on the map.

Can you describe Shirley's route to school?

What does she pass on the journey?

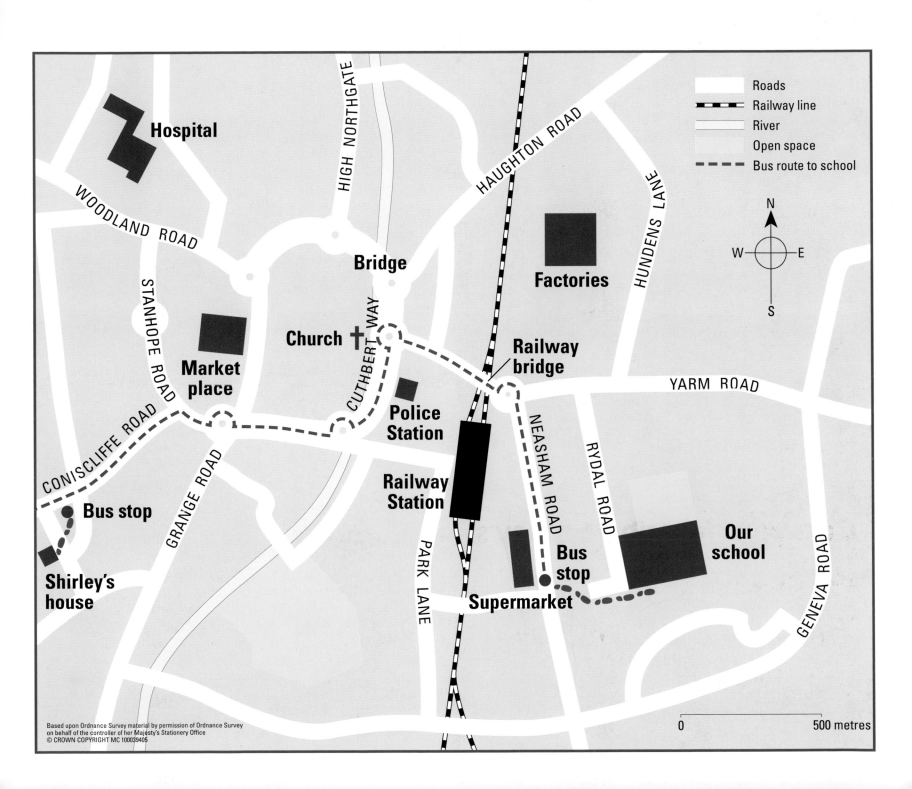

Roads
Railway line
River
Open space
Bus route to school

Hospital

WOODLAND ROAD

HIGH NORTHGATE

HAUGHTON ROAD

Bridge

Factories

HUNDENS LANE

N
W E
S

STANHOPE ROAD

Church

CUTHBERT WAY

Railway bridge

YARM ROAD

Market place

CONISCLIFFE ROAD

Police Station

NEASHAM ROAD

RYDAL ROAD

Bus stop

GRANGE ROAD

Railway Station

Our school

GENEVA ROAD

Shirley's house

PARK LANE

Bus stop

Supermarket

Based upon Ordnance Survey material by permission of Ordnance Survey
on behalf of the controller of her Majesty's Stationery Office
© CROWN COPYRIGHT MC 100039405

0   500 metres

21

Further information for Parents and Teachers

JOURNEY TO SCHOOL ACTIVITY PAGE

Use the activities on these pages to help you to make the most of *Journey to School* in your classroom.

Activities suggested on this page support progression in learning by consolidating and developing ideas from the book and helping the children to link the new concepts with their own experiences. Making these links is crucial in helping young children to engage with learning and to become lifelong learners.

Ideas on the next page develop essential skills for learning by suggesting ways of making links across the curriculum and in particular to literacy, numeracy and ICT.

WORD PANEL

Check that the children know the meaning of each of these words from the book.

buildings	local area	plan
county	luggage	postcode
flat	outside	roundabout
journey		

USING MAPS

Use an internet search engine to find maps at different scales as well as aerial photographs of where you live. Some internet maps show both photographs and maps that can be superimposed upon each other. This is often available for bigger cities.

- Compare the maps. Find similarities and differences between them. Talk to the children about why the maps are the same and different. Discuss which maps you might use for which purposes.
- Compare the aerial photographs with the maps. Talk about information which is shown on one, but not on the other. Talk about different reasons for using photographs and maps.
- Ask children to draw what they think an aerial picture of the school might look like. If possible, compare their drawings to a real aerial picture.

FINDING DIRECTIONS

Identify a short, safe walk the children can do. Use an internet route finder to print out directions, maps and photographs of locations and landmarks on your route.

- Plan a walk together. On your risk-assessment, try to plan for a ratio of between 1:6 and 1:2, depending on your class and the route.
- Let the children walk in small groups, each with an adult. Allow the children within each group to take different kinds of route finders: directions, maps and photographs.
- Let some children take photographs to record your walk.
- After the walk, talk to the children about which they prefer using: directions, maps or photographs. Discuss the fact that different adults like using different route finders too!
- Let children work in their groups to annotate their route finders and write about what they observed. Make a display using the route finders, children's own photographs and their writing.

MAKING A ROUTE FINDER

Challenge children to create a route finder of their own journey to school. They could do this using directions, maps or photographs.

- Children who live a short distance away can draw their own maps.
- Those living further away could print out a map and annotate it to show their journey to school.
- If children can't take photographs, suggest that they draw landmarks and locations in the order that they pass them.

USING PLANS

Challenge children to draw a plan of your school like the one on pages 10 -11. Remind them to include:

- Your classroom and other classrooms
- Toilet and cloakroom areas
- The playground
- The head teacher's office and the front office
- Assembly hall or dining room.
- Other important rooms such as computer suite or library. Identify one part of the plan - perhaps it could be your classroom or part of the school grounds. Create a larger sized plan of that part of the school. Let children use your plan to explore different ways of using the space.
- How would they like the classroom to be organised? Remind them what must be in the classroom and identify fixed features like the doors, windows, interactive whiteboard.
- Ask them to plan an environmental area or an adventure playground. Perhaps they could zone the playground.

USING JOURNEY TO SCHOOL FOR CROSS CURRICULAR WORK

The revised national curriculum focuses on children developing key competencies as

- successful learners
- confident individuals and
- responsible citizens.

Cross curricular work is particularly beneficial in developing the thinking and learning skills that contribute to building these competencies because it encourages children to make links, to transfer learning skills and to apply knowledge from one context to another. As importantly, cross curricular work can help children to understand how school work links to their daily lives. For many children, this is a key motivation in becoming a learner.

The web below indicates some areas for cross curricular study. Others may well come from your own class's engagement with the ideas in the book.

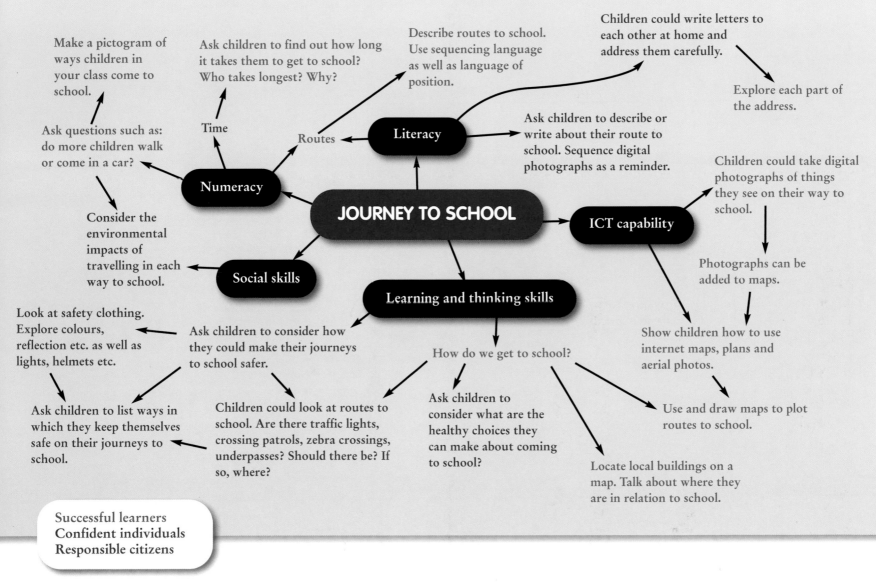

Make a pictogram of ways children in your class come to school.

Ask questions such as: do more children walk or come in a car?

Consider the environmental impacts of travelling in each way to school.

Ask children to find out how long it takes them to get to school? Who takes longest? Why?

Time

Routes

Numeracy

Social skills

Describe routes to school. Use sequencing language as well as language of position.

Literacy

JOURNEY TO SCHOOL

Ask children to describe or write about their route to school. Sequence digital photographs as a reminder.

Children could write letters to each other at home and address them carefully.

Explore each part of the address.

Children could take digital photographs of things they see on their way to school.

ICT capability

Photographs can be added to maps.

Learning and thinking skills

Look at safety clothing. Explore colours, reflection etc. as well as lights, helmets etc.

Ask children to consider how they could make their journeys to school safer.

Ask children to list ways in which they keep themselves safe on their journeys to school.

Children could look at routes to school. Are there traffic lights, crossing patrols, zebra crossings, underpasses? Should there be? If so, where?

How do we get to school?

Ask children to consider what are the healthy choices they can make about coming to school?

Show children how to use internet maps, plans and aerial photos.

Use and draw maps to plot routes to school.

Locate local buildings on a map. Talk about where they are in relation to school.

Successful learners
Confident individuals
Responsible citizens

23

Index